the Swiftie Bucket List

101 Must-Have Moments for Taylor Swift Fans

BLUESTONE BOOKS

Table of Contents

101 Ways to Be a Swiftie! 9
#**1** Experience the Eras Tour........................... 10
#**2** Embrace Your "willow" Coven 11
#**3** Walk Cornelia Street So Taylor Doesn't Have To......... 12
#**4** Make & Share Friendship Bracelets the Taylor Way 13
#**5** Prepare High Tea................................... 14
#**6** Get an Eras Manicure............................... 15
#**7** Stand Up for Somebody 16
#**8** Catch Up on the Classics: *The Great Gatsby*............. 17
#**9** Plant a Memory Garden............................. 18
#**10** Break Your Favorite Toys............................ 19
#**11** Have a Listening Party.............................. 20
#**12** Watch Taylor's Movies............................... 22
#**13** Make Thirteen Your Lucky Number 23
#**14** Make the Whole Place Shimmer...................... 24
#**15** Take a Taylor "Dead Day"............................ 25
#**16** Do Good Taylor Style................................ 26
#**17** Get to Know "Holiday House"........................ 28
#**18** Catch Up on the Classics: *Jane Eyre* 29
#**19** Do a Crossword Puzzle............................. 30
#**20** Dye Your Hair Pastel................................ 31
#**21** Go "Back to December"............................. 32
#**22** Wear Their Initial on a Chain 'Round Your Neck 33
#**23** Cry at a Taylor Swift Song 34
#**24** Kiss in the Rain.................................... 36
#**25** Dress Up Like Taylor for Halloween 37
#**26** Have "The Best Day" 38

#27 Enjoy a Cupcake for One 39
#28 Catch Up on the Classics: "The Albatross" 40
#29 Bake Cinnamon Buns............................. 41
#30 Write a Love Story 42
#31 Play *Grand Theft Auto*............................ 44
#32 Catch Up on the Classics: *Little Women* 45
#33 Make Midnights Your Mornings 46
#34 Eat at Olive Garden............................... 47
#35 Binge-Watch Friends 48
#36 Knit a Scarf...................................... 50
#37 Discover Your Aura............................... 51
#38 Catch Up on the Classics: *Romeo & Juliet*............. 52
#39 Go to an Arcade 53
#40 Rewrite a Taylor Song............................ 54
#41 Reinvent Yourself................................ 56
#42 Make a Fort..................................... 57
#43 Watch Rugby in a Pub 58
#44 Drink Starbucks 59
#45 Watch the Big-Screen Inspiration 60
#46 Create Swiftie Fan Art............................ 62
#47 Surprise Someone Special 63
#48 Catch Up on the Classics: *A Streetcar Named Desire* 64
#49 Talk the Talk.................................... 65
#50 Write a Fairy Tale................................ 66
#51 Listen to Taylor on Vinyl.......................... 68
#52 Catch Up on the Classics: *The Wonderful Wizard of Oz* ... 69
#53 Strike a Match on a Picture to Burn 70
#54 Book the Night Train............................. 71
#55 Marry Someone with Paper Rings.................. 72
#56 Wear Cowboy Boots.............................. 73
#57 Get Your Boating License 74

#58 Catch Up on the Classics: *The Scarlet Letter* 75

#59 Write a Breakup Song 76

#60 Find Her Easter Eggs 78

#61 Turn Up that Location Ballad 79

#62 Make a Taylor Swift Vision Board 80

#63 Go Full Taylor Glam 81

#64 Be Generous with Your Time 82

#65 Take a Taylor-Inspired Road Trip. 83

#66 Take Polaroids 84

#67 Go to a Christmas Tree Farm 86

#68 Catch Up on the Classics: *The Sun Also Rises* 87

#69 Turn a Skeptic into a Swiftie 88

#70 Do Something Someone Says You Can't Do 89

#71 Write a Poem. 90

#72 Catch Up on the Classics: "The Road Not Taken" 92

#73 Do Something Bad 93

#74 Have a Merry Swiftmas. 94

#75 Use a Typewriter. 95

#76 Speak Exclusively in Taylor's Vocabulary 96

#77 Listen to Songs Taylor Wrote but Didn't Sing 98

#78 Catch Up on the Classics: *A Tale of Two Cities* 99

#79 Make Cats Your Whole Personality 100

#80 Leave the Christmas Lights Up 'Til January. 101

#81 Write a Revenge Fantasy 102

#82 Embrace the Snakes. 104

#83 Take on an English Accent. 105

#84 Get to Know that James Dean Daydream 106

#85 Read All the Books Beside Your Bed 107

#86 Offset Your Carbon Footprint. 108

#87 Catch Up on the Classics: *A Wrinkle in Time* 109

#88 Learn Words in Other Languages 110

#89 Watch a Magic Show 111

#**90** Write a Heartfelt Song	112
#**91** Cheer On Your Favorite Football Team	113
#**92** Catch Up on the Classics: *Alice's Adventures in Wonderland*	114
#**93** Stand Up for LGBTQ+ Friends and Strangers	115
#**94** Memorize Her Dance Routines	116
#**95** Use "All Too Well (10 Minute Version)" as a Timer	117
#**96** Dedicate a Song	118
#**97** Crash a Party	120
#**98** Catch Up on the Classics: *Rebecca*	121
#**99** Drop Your Own Clues Before Making a Big Announcement	122
#**100** Listen to Taylor's Latest Album	123
#**101** Make a Song-of-the-Day Calendar	124

101 Ways to Be a Swiftie!

Because thirteen ways would just be too few. Check off *The Swiftie Bucket List* as you live out a wonderstruck time of celebrating the music, the myths, and the fandom of the unstoppable Taylorverse. Discover 101 must-have moments and activities inspired by Taylor Swift's favorite things, her chameleonic transformations, her kind heart, and the Swiftie society she's created.

Whether you've been listening to Taylor since she picked up her first twelve-string or you couldn't fight the magnetic draw of her revolutionary Eras Tour, this bucket list is packed with creative and inspiring challenges to make your Swiftie wishes come true.

Take cues from her lyrics and life by reading the books she hints at in her songs, leaving the Christmas lights up 'til January, and making midnights your mornings. Don't be shy in following Taylor's lead when you find your itty bitty kitty committee, drink Starbucks, kiss in the rain, and have a Merry Swiftmas. Turn a skeptic into a Swiftie, stand up for somebody, and be generous—just like Taylor.

Spark unforgettable memories as you check off this ultimate bucket list of Miss Americana-style adventures you'll never forget. So grab your friends, embrace the eras, and start checking off your goals. Because every fan deserves to live out their wildest Swiftie dreams!

#1 Experience the Eras Tour

There's more than one way to let the incomparable glow of the Eras Tour fill you with dazzling light. Taylor made sure no Swiftie could be left behind, and in addition to live concerts that set off earthquake readers, she also released the tour in movie theaters and on streaming services.

Which was your Eras Tour?

- [x] Created a spectacle unlike any other in my living room
- [x] Stood in a local theater singing with strangers
- [x] Taylor-gated outside a nearby Eras Tour concert
- [x] Shared friendship bracelets from the live show!
- [x] Flew across the world to a new city

What did the Eras Tour mean to you?

_____
_____
_____

What are your takeaways from her eras in the show?

_____
_____
_____

#2 Embrace Your "willow" Coven

During the Eras Tour, the song "willow" unraveled across the stage almost like a ballet—if the ballerinas were beautiful witches wielding glowing orbs in a mystical woodland. But you don't have to travel deep into the woods to find your coven. Connect with Swifties in your area to gush about your love of Taylor or discuss the meaning of her lyrics.

Y/N I teamed up with Swifties I know

Y/N I teamed up with some Swifties who are new to me

Y/N We shared friendship bracelets

I was surprised that...

_____
_____
_____

It made me feel part of something special when...

_____
_____
_____

11

#3 Walk Cornelia Street So Taylor Doesn't Have To

Taylor name-drops locations in her songs more than a little. And she mentions street names, parks, and neighborhoods enough to make them the target of wandering Swifties in dozens of cities all over the world. Go on a stroll in these destinations and see what you observe. Do you feel a little closer to Taylor and the meaning of her songs?

- ◯ Georgia from "Tim McGraw" off of *Taylor Swift*
- ◯ Cornelia Street from "Cornelia Street" off of *Lover*
- ◯ 16th Avenue from "I Think He Knows" off of *Lover*
- ◯ Camden Market from "London Boy" off of *Lover*
- ◯ The intersection of Sunset Boulevard and Vine Street in Los Angeles, California, from "Gorgeous" off of *Reputation*
- ◯ Centennial Park in Nashville, Tennessee, from "invisible string" off of *folklore*
- ◯ The High Line in New York from "cardigan" off of *folklore*
- ◯ Tupelo, Mississippi, from "Dorothea" off of *evermore*
- ◯ The Black Dog bar in London from "The Black Dog" off of *The Tortured Poets Department*
- ◯ The Chelsea Hotel in New York from "The Tortured Poets Department" off of *The Tortured Poets Department*

#4 Make & Share Friendship Bracelets the Taylor Way

Friendship bracelets came back with a vengeance after Taylor mentioned them in the bridge of "You're On Your Own Kid" off of her tenth album *Midnights*. "So make the friendship bracelets / take the moment and taste it / you've got no reason to be afraid." It's an inspiring message to cherish the people and moments that matter. So inspiring that it's now standard to make friendship bracelets with lyrics and wishes before a Taylor Swift event and share them with other Swifties.

Have you traded friendship bracelets? What messages, lyrics, or manifestations did you create on your own bracelet or see on others? If you haven't made one yet, make a list of the phrases you'd like to see on yours!

_____
_____
_____
_____
_____
_____
_____
_____
_____
_____

L O V E R

#5 Prepare High Tea

In "London Boy" off of *Lover*, Taylor reminisces on all the things she likes about London and the typical English customs she's enjoyed there. She specifically mentions "high tea," which is more than just a bag put into a tea cup. It's a beautiful afternoon teatime experience complete with freshly steeped tea leaves and a tower of tiny sweets and sandwiches. Find a tea room near you that prepares high tea, or create your own!

What was on your high tea tower?

What was special about the experience?

Do you think you take your tea like Taylor?

#6 Get an Eras Manicure

During the Eras Tour, Taylor was spotted with ten different colors on each of her nails to represent ten of her albums. Do a spa day the Taylor way and get your nails done. Choose the colors that best reflect ten of your favorite albums. One way to boost this experience is to layer each nail with a sticker or a painted image representing the album (snakes and butterflies, anyone?).

Whether you do your manicure at home or at a salon, make a list of the colors and flourishes you'd want to see on your nails.

#7 Stand Up for Somebody

Taylor is a force for good, and she doesn't shy away when it comes to standing up for friends and strangers. In 2016, Taylor helped out fellow singer Kesha by donating $250,000 to Kesha's legal fees for a court case against her former producer. In 2017, she won her own case against a radio DJ who made inappropriate advances on her. She asked for just $1 in damages as a symbolic way to speak out for all those who have ever been worried to speak up when their boundaries have been crossed.

Not everyone feels comfortable speaking up when they need help, or they may need the support of a strong ally by their side.

When have you felt this way and had someone support you?

_____
_____
_____
_____
_____
_____
_____
_____

#8 Catch Up on the Classics: *The Great Gatsby*

The Great Gatsby by F. Scott Fitzgerald

Taylor sneaks literary references into many of her songs. The song "happiness" off of *evermore* includes a line recalling this great American novel. Possibly referring to her partner's next girlfriend, Taylor sings, "And I hope she'll be a beautiful fool," not unlike the Fitzgerald character Daisy, who says, "I hope she'll be a fool—that's the best thing a girl can be in this world, a beautiful little fool."

Y/N Read the book

Y/N Watched the movie

Imagine it through Taylor's eyes and write down your thoughts.

_____
_____
_____
_____
_____
_____
_____

#9 Plant a Memory Garden

In her song, "The Great War," off of *Midnights*, Taylor uses historical imagery to think back on a difficult point in a relationship and how they made it through. She says the line, "plant a memory garden," which may be metaphorical or literal. Decide what kind of memory garden you'd like to make. Is it flowers? Photos? Is it memories of your favorite Taylor moments, or is it something more personal to you? Map it out here.

#10 Break Your Favorite Toys

The Tortured Poets Department includes a track called "My Boy Only Breaks His Favorite Toys" in which she describes a boyfriend's bad behavior. She uses the metaphors of him breaking his favorite toys and smashing her sandcastles. Turn the tables! Build a sandcastle and then smash it all down. Find unusable toys from the depths of your childhood toybox or basement, and smash those too. (Donate any toys that are in good condition to a local charity.)

Smash it all up and describe or draw the feeling afterward.

#11 Have a Listening Party

Got fifteen hours on you? Go full marathon mode. Queue up Taylor Swift and listen all the way through *The Tortured Poets Department* and beyond. Open up those vault tracks, watch the short films, and let yourself feel the feels.

◯ *Taylor Swift*

◯ *Fearless*

◯ *Speak Now*

◯ *Red*

◯ *1989*

◯ *Reputation*

◯ *Lover*

◯ *folklore*

◯ *evermore*

○ *Midnights*

○ *The Tortured Poets Department*

○

Circle your favorite albums. What do they mean to you?

#12 Watch Taylor's Movies

Taylor has been polishing her acting chops ever since she first appeared on television's *CSI* back in 2009. Get the popcorn popping and see if you can spot her in any of these movies.

◯ *Amsterdam*, 2022, as Liz Meekins
◯ *Cats*, 2019, as Bombalurina
◯ *The Giver*, 2014, as Rosemary
◯ *The Lorax*, 2012, as Audrey
◯ *Valentine's Day*, 2010, as Felicia

Which character is your favorite? Do you prefer watching Taylor in her own music videos or on the big screen?

#13 Make Thirteen Your Lucky Number

Before Taylor, the number thirteen was associated with bad luck. Now Friday the 13th and December 13th (Taylor's birthday) are lucky days. It's her favorite number, and somehow good things always seem to come up thirteen!

Make a list of thirteen things that bring you luck or have made you feel lucky.

1. _____
2. _____
3. _____
4. _____
5. _____
6. _____
7. _____
8. _____
9. _____
10. _____
11. _____
12. _____
13. _____

#14 Make the Whole Place Shimmer

Dazzle like Taylor! The song "Bejeweled" from *Midnights* inspired fans at the Eras Tour to bedazzle and bejewel their clothing. Craft something sparkly, whether it's jewelry, jean jackets, hats, shoes, or your own fashion that feels Taylor-made.

Draw what it'll look like below or write a description of how you got your inspiration.

#15 Take a Taylor "Dead Day"

There's no question that performing for three hours on stage every night requires strength, stamina, and a nourishing diet. But even Taylor has her self-described "dead days" when she lounges around and snacks from her bed. She calls these days a "dream scenario" and a way to reward herself for her hard work.

What's your favorite way to pass the time on a "dead day"?

_____

_____

_____

_____

_____

How do you reward yourself for a job well done?

_____

_____

_____

_____

_____

_____

_____

_____

#16 Do Good Taylor Style

Be a giver! Taylor is known for her charitable work and support of the underdog when they need it most. When you're a superstar, money can go a long way, but it's not the only way you can help a stranger or a friend in need. Here are ways you can do good for others just like Taylor. Have you done any of them?

- Collect and donate money for a cause that's important to you
- Donate books you no longer read to local libraries, schools, or charities
- Volunteer in your free time at a local hospital, soup kitchen, church, or event that supports causes that matter to you
- Lend a helping hand
- Show up for your friends and speak up for people who need it

Date	Good Deed	How It Made Me Feel to Help

#17 Get to Know "Holiday House"

The song, "The Last Great American Dynasty" from *folklore* is inspired by Rebekah Harkness, the former owner of Taylor's Rhode Island home. Taylor has said that Rebekah's legacy of always causing a stir in the town felt familiar. Listen to the song and read more about the lore behind Holiday House. While you can't visit Taylor's home in Watch Hill, you can tour local mansions in Westerly and Newport, Rhode Island, that all come with their own histories (and even scandals).

What do you know about "Holiday House"?

_____
_____
_____
_____
_____

What is another place you know that feels like it has a life of its own?

_____
_____
_____
_____
_____
_____
_____

#18 Catch Up on the Classics: *Jane Eyre*

Jane Eyre by Charlotte Brontë

Taylor sneaks literary references into many of her songs. "invisible string" off of *folklore* shares ideas from Brontë's book when Edward Rochester tells Jane, "I have a strange feeling with regard to you. As if I had a string somewhere under my left ribs, tightly knotted to a similar string in you."

Y/N Read the book

Y/N Watched the movie

Imagine it through Taylor's eyes and write down your thoughts.

_____
_____
_____
_____
_____
_____
_____

#19 Do a Crossword Puzzle

Taylor's song "Red" off of the album of the same name talks about messy love sometimes feeling like a crossword with no right answer. Find a Swiftie crossword puzzle online or in a bookstore and do it up! Here's a mini version to get you started:

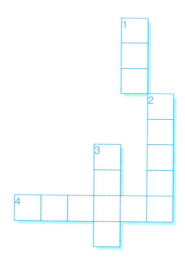

Down

1. Taylor's favorite lip color.
2. An album with pastel colors.
3. The ones she always goes home to.

Across

4. She owns one of these with a koi fish detail.

#20 Dye Your Hair Pastel

Taylor Swift loves, *loves* colors. She named a whole album after the color red. She talks about feelings and people as being blue or gold. When she felt her lowest professionally, she came back with a vengeance—and in black and white—with *Reputation*. Taylor embraced pastels when she wrote *Lover*. In her promos and music videos, her blonde hair was feathered with blue and pink tips. Get on board with Taylor's playful side and dye your own hair. The best part is, you can choose a temporary dye if you don't want to commit!

If you're paying tribute to Taylor with your hair, which color are you choosing?

_____

_____

_____

What are your favorite lines in Taylor's music that talk about color?

_____

_____

_____

_____

_____

_____

_____

_____

#21 Go "Back to December"

Plenty of people accuse Taylor of just writing breakup songs about the boyfriends who wronged her. Any Swiftie knows this just isn't true. More importantly, she's been mature enough to write about when she's wronged someone else or made a mistake. Songs like "The Great War" and "Afterglow" do just that. So does "Back to December," a bittersweet breakup song about realizing she let a good one go.

Which Taylor songs help you process your mistakes or appreciate someone better?

#22 Wear Their Initial on a Chain 'Round Your Neck

Taylor loves a true-to-life detail in her songs to express something bigger. She's able to take something simple, like a scarf, and give it meaning. And speaking of things that go around your neck, Taylor loves scattering references to necklaces and lockets around her songs like diamonds. She mentions lockets in *Red* and *Reputation*, necklaces around her or her lover's necks in *1989*, and wearing their initial around her neck in the song "Call It What You Want." She wore a "J," in the music video for "Delicate."

What kind of necklace would you wear as a secret nod to something you care about?

_____

_____

_____

_____

What kind of jewelry lets you show off your Swiftie status?

_____

_____

_____

_____

_____

#23 Cry at a Taylor Swift Song

Taylor may have had teardrops on her guitar, but everyone else has had them streaming down their faces. Whether it's songs about heartbreak, loss, illness, regret, or even hope, Blondie knows how to make a deep cut. Which of these songs hits you hard?

◯ "The Best Day" *(Fearless)*

◯ "Dear John" *(Speak Now)*

◯ "Back to December" *(Speak Now)*

◯ "All Too Well (10 Minute Version)" *(Red)*

◯ "Ronan" *(Red)*

◯ "Clean" *(1989)*

◯ "Soon You'll Get Better" *(Lover)*

◯ "exile" *(folklore)*

◯ "my tears ricochet" *(folklore)*

💧 "champagne problems" (*evermore*)

💧 "happiness" (*evermore*)

💧 "tolerate it" (*evermore*)

💧 "marjorie" (*evermore*)

💧 "Bigger Than The Whole Sky" (*Midnights*)

💧 "So Long, London" (*The Tortured Poets Department*)

💧 "loml" (*The Tortured Poets Department*)

What other songs bring on the waterworks for you?

#24 Kiss in the Rain

If the Eras Tour was any indication, a little rain never stopped Taylor from doing anything, and certainly not from performing her heart out or making grand romantic gestures. Taylor talks about the magic of kissing in the rain in her song, "The Way I Loved You," on the *Fearless* album. Write down a memory or a fantasy of kissing someone in the rain.

#25 Dress Up Like Taylor for Halloween

Choose your favorite Taylor era (or combine two or more!) and make her style your own for Halloween. Whether your costume is full glam, crafty homemade, or classic cowboy, there's almost no end to how you can achieve iconic Taylor style. What are the must-haves for your favorite Taylor look?

#26 Have "The Best Day"

Spend a day with someone you love. In the song "Best Day" off of *Fearless*, Taylor sings about how special days with her mom carried her through bad days and tough moments when she was young. Whether it's a parent, a sibling, or a member of your chosen family, who would you spend the day with? Plan out what you'll do, and see if you connect any of the lyrics in this song with this experience.

_____
_____
_____
_____
_____
_____
_____
_____
_____
_____
_____
_____
_____

#27 Enjoy a Cupcake for One

Sometimes, celebrating yourself is exactly what you need! Taylor once posted a picture of a sweet treat on social media and captioned it "Cupcake for One." Take yourself out on a date for a cupcake, a dessert, or something that makes you feel rewarded.

What's your treat of choice?

_____
_____
_____

What about doing something just for you and no one else feels empowering?

_____
_____
_____
_____
_____
_____
_____
_____
_____
_____

#28 Catch Up on the Classics: "The Albatross"

"L'Albatros" by Charles Baudelaire or "The Rime of the Ancient Mariner" by Samuel Taylor Coleridge

Taylor sneaks literary references into many of her songs. In the song "The Albatross" off of *The Tortured Poets Department*, she likens herself to the misunderstood, larger-than-life bird depicted in classic poetry.

Y/N Read the poem(s)

Imagine it through Taylor's eyes and write down your thoughts.

_____
_____
_____
_____
_____
_____
_____
_____
_____

#29 Bake Cinnamon Buns

Get baking! Taylor loves baking for her friends and as a way to relax. She bakes cookies and bread, in particular, but cinnamon buns are her go-to. Write down a cinnamon bun recipe here and rate it. Is it Taylor-worthy?

Ingredients List

Steps

Rating

#30 Write a Love Story

Baby, just say yes. Capture the passion of an epic romance the Taylor way, like she does in her song "Love Story" off of *Speak Now*. Write the premise of a love story here.

_____
_____
_____
_____
_____
_____
_____
_____
_____
_____
_____
_____
_____
_____
_____
_____
_____
_____
_____

#31 Play *Grand Theft Auto*

Taylor refers to the video game *Grand Theft Auto* in "So High School" from *The Tortured Poets Department*. Play the game or watch videos of people playing it online.

What about the video game feels similar to or different from Taylor's attitude?

#32 Catch Up on the Classics: *Little Women*

Little Women by Louisa May Alcott

Taylor sneaks literary references into many of her songs. Taylor sings the line "she fell through the ice, then came out alive" in the song, "The Bolter," off of *The Tortured Poets Department*. The very same happens to the character Amy March in the book *Little Women*. Other lines, like "a curious child, ever reviled / by everyone except her own father" line up with how readers have felt about Amy's character in the book.

Y/N Read the book

Y/N Watched the movie

Imagine it through Taylor's eyes and write down your thoughts.

_____
_____
_____
_____
_____
_____
_____

#33 Make Midnights Your Mornings

Blondie loves a midnight. Even before the album *Midnights*, Taylor was singing about the freedom of midnights. Whether it's doing what you want because no one else is watching, trying something unusual because you're swept up and in love, feeling deep feelings, or lying wide awake in contemplation, there's something about midnights that's private and liberating all at once. Which of these song-inspired midnights have you tried out for fun?

My midnights

- ◯ Breakfast at midnight ("22")
- ◯ Coffee at midnight ("You Are In Love")
- ◯ Stare out at the midnight sea ("The Last Great American Dynasty")
- ◯ Wear a dress at midnight ("happiness")
- ◯ Meet at midnight ("Lavender Haze")
- ◯ Midnights become afternoons ("Anti-Hero")
- ◯ Change like midnight ("Midnight Rain")

#34 Eat at Olive Garden

Taylor references the Italian-American restaurant in her song "no body, no crime" on the album *evermore*. While the song is something of a murder-mystery ballad, Taylor has a way of incorporating everyday habits, details, and places (like Olive Garden) into her songs in a way that makes the song feel real to us.

What other places, spaces, or ideas stick out to you in her music?

#35 Binge-Watch *Friends*

Taylor has said on many occasions that her favorite comfort show is *Friends*. But did you know there are lyrics that line up to actual scenes in *Friends*, too? Binge-watch the show for yourself and see if you can spot them.

Friends

Phoebe sings, "There was a girl, we'll call her 'Betty'"

Janice says, "You, Mr. Right Place at the Right Time"

Phoebe says, "I bet she's looking up at us and smiling right now... Oh, she's in hell for sure."

Ross says, "Thank you, Amy"

Joey says, "So I didn't know that, but you should see your faces"

Taylor

- "Betty" is a song off of *folklore*

- "Mister always at the right place at the right time" in "Mr. Perfectly Fine"

- Taylor sings, "I bet she's laughing up at us from hell" in "Anti-Hero"

- Taylor titled a song, "ThanK you aIMee"

- Taylor sings, "No I'm not, but you should see your faces" in "But Daddy I Love Him"

#36 Knit a Scarf

If "All Too Well" from *Red* taught Swifties anything, it's that scarves are a must-have accessory. Find a knitting book or YouTube video to teach you how to knit a scarf or an article of clothing that reminds you of Taylor. Sketch it out here, or write about what learning something new or the art of knitting means to you.

#37 Discover Your Aura

In the song "Bejeweled" off of *Midnights*, Taylor sings about someone telling her that her aura is the color of moonstone. Read about auras online and learn how to find yours, or seek out someone who specializes in auras to tell you yours.

What color is your aura?

_____
_____
_____

What does this color mean?

_____
_____
_____
_____
_____
_____
_____
_____
_____
_____
_____
_____
_____

#38 Catch Up on the Classics: *Romeo & Juliet*

Romeo & Juliet by William Shakespeare

Taylor sneaks literary references into many of her songs. In "Love Story" off of *Fearless*, Taylor sings "you were Romeo, you were throwing pebbles," and "And my Daddy said 'Stay away from Juliet,'" giving listeners a look into the famous play's doomed romance.

Y/N Saw the play

Y/N Read the book

Y/N Watched the movie

Imagine it through Taylor's eyes and write down your thoughts.

_____
_____
_____
_____
_____
_____
_____

#39 Go to an Arcade

The song "coney island" off of *evermore* is a sad breakup song that's set in a place known for its entertainment. Take a cue from this song, but make it fun. Go to an arcade near you and play for keeps.

What are you playing?

What about this song makes you think?

What are your favorite ways to escape?

#40 Rewrite a Taylor Song

Choose one of your favorite T-Swift songs. Rewrite the lyrics below, but include details that are meaningful to your own life.

#41 Reinvent Yourself

Taylor knows how to reinvent her image. Whether it was learning how to transition from country to pop or coming back from the dead when her reputation was in the gutter, she's got a magical ability to shapeshift.

How would you reinvent yourself if you could?

_____
_____
_____
_____
_____
_____
_____

What alter ego would you pursue?

_____
_____
_____
_____
_____
_____
_____
_____
_____
_____

#42 Make a Fort

In "Call It What You Want" on *Reputation*, Taylor sings about "makin' forts under covers" as a reference to the playfulness of being in love. Make a fort in your own space, whether that's under the covers of your bed or in your living room. Design it here.

#43 Watch Rugby in a Pub

Like Taylor Swift hanging out with her "London Boy" and his friends in a pub on her album, *Lover*, you can do the same! Catch a rugby match and get hyped up by the excitement of the fans around you.

Have you watched or played rugby before?

Y/N

What teams are playing?

What about this detail in the song makes it more relatable?

#44 Drink Starbucks

Swifties know that Taylor doesn't dare call Starbucks a guilty pleasure: it's a lifestyle. In the past, she's been devoted to vanilla lattes, but she's also been spotted drinking maple or pumpkin spice lattes (she's an autumn girl at heart). Place your latte order here.

#45 Watch the Big-Screen Inspiration

Taylor name-drops and alludes to different films and television shows in some of her songs. Have you seen these films and shows?

Y/N *The Great Escape* (1960): A film namedropped in "Getaway Car" on *Reputation*

Y/N *Who's Afraid of Virginia Woolf* (1966): A film title that may have influenced "Who's Afraid of Little Old Me" off of *The Tortured Poets Department*

Y/N *Bonnie & Clyde* (1967): A film namedropped in "Getaway Car" on *Reputation*

Y/N *The Little Mermaid* (1989): Ariel says the phrase, "But Daddy I Love Him" just like the song off of *The Tortured Poets Department*.

Y/N *The Notebook* (2004): Allie says the phrase, "But Daddy I Love Him" just like the song off of *The Tortured Poets Department*.

_____

_____

Y/N *Prison Break* (2005): A television series namedropped in "Getaway Car" on *Reputation*

_____

_____

Y/N *Mad Men* (2007): Taylor has said that she first heard the phrase "Lavender Haze" from *Midnights* spoken in an episode of this series called "The Mountain King."

_____

_____

Y/N *Where the Crawdads Sing* (2022): Taylor wrote the song "Carolina."

_____

_____

#46 Create Swiftie Fan Art

The Eras Tour saw some of the most impressive fan art ever imagined. But spend any time on Etsy and you know there's no wrong way to express yourself as a Swiftie.

What's your favorite kind of fan art you've seen?

_____
_____
_____

If you've created you own fan art, describe it here.

_____
_____
_____
_____

If you haven't, what would you make if you could?

_____
_____
_____
_____

#47 Surprise Someone Special

No one loves her fans quite like Taylor. Over the years, she has shown up to engagement parties, bridal showers, weddings, birthday parties, and get-togethers to show her Swifties the love. And she doesn't just stop by. She comes toting hand-painted crafts, cookies she's personally baked, recipes, and generous gifts. What makes these moments so inspiring is the thoughtfulness that goes into it. Like a good friend or family member, she makes sure that when she shows up, she's present.

In what ways could you surprise someone in your life that would make their day?

_____

_____

_____

_____

How has someone else's thoughtfulness made you feel seen?

_____

_____

_____

_____

_____

_____

_____

#48 Catch Up on the Classics: *A Streetcar Named Desire*

A Streetcar Named Desire by Tennessee Williams

Taylor sneaks literary references into many of her songs. In "Hits Different" off of *Midnights*, there are parallels to Blanche DuBois's character in the final scene of the play as she is mentally unraveling and believes her lover has returned to her. Taylor's version says, "Is that your key in the door? / Is it okay? Is it you? / Or have they come to take me away?"

Y/N Saw the play

Y/N Read the play

Y/N Watched the movie

Imagine it through Taylor's eyes and write down your thoughts.

_____

_____

_____

_____

#49 Talk the Talk

Memorize something Taylor has said that's full of your kind of wisdom—whether it's a speech, a statement, or a chorus from her song—and make it your mantra. Start by writing it out here and come back to it over and over when you need a boost.

#50 Write a Fairy Tale

There is seemingly no end to Taylor's fairy tale world in her music. Songs like "White Horse," "Enchanted," and "Today Was a Fairy Tale" remind listeners about the excitement and pitfalls of fairy tales. Write the premise of a Swiftian fairy tale here.

#51 Listen to Taylor on Vinyl

Record players didn't make a comeback just to sit and collect dust. Everything sounds better on vinyl records, and especially Taylor. You can put each of her albums—and some with special editions—on the turntables and shake it off or get down bad however you please. Many of these include special liner notes that aren't released with any other format.

Which of Taylor's music have you listened to on a record player?

_____
_____
_____
_____
_____
_____
_____

How have her liner notes or special additions made you understand her music better?

_____
_____
_____
_____
_____
_____

#52 Catch Up on the Classics: *The Wonderful Wizard of Oz*

The Wonderful Wizard of Oz by L. Frank Baum

Taylor sneaks literary references into many of her songs. In "loml" off of *The Tortured Poets Department*, Taylor sings, "The coward claimed he was a lion." The "cowardly lion" is a reference to the lion in the book *The Wonderful Wizard of Oz* and its movie tie-in.

Y/N Read the book

Y/N Watched the movie

Y/N Saw the play

Imagine it through Taylor's eyes and write down your thoughts.

_____
_____
_____
_____
_____

#53 Strike a Match on a Picture to Burn

Taylor came out of the gate as an artist with a fiery attitude. She sang "Picture to Burn" on her self-titled debut album. In true country-revenge-song fashion, Taylor sings an upbeat but fierce diatribe about an ex who wronged her, promising to light a match and burn the memory of the relationship. As an artist who's always had a way of tapping into universal feelings, this song is a fun revenge fantasy that lets listeners channel their own versions.

What picture would you symbolically burn?

_____
_____
_____
_____

What about the attitude of this song makes this song so fun for Swifties?

_____
_____
_____
_____
_____
_____
_____

#54 Book the Night Train

If you're Taylor, you book the night train to sit in your feelings as you mull over "champagne problems." The first line of this song on *evermore* sets up the idea of a solemn train ride, but if you're a Swiftie, you know that the train ride could be spent listening to hours of Taylor herself.

What would you do with hours on a night train?

_____
_____
_____
_____
_____
_____
_____
_____
_____
_____
_____
_____
_____

#55 Marry Someone with Paper Rings

You can glitter and shimmer with shiny things, but true love is "Paper Rings." In this track on *Lover*, Taylor sings about the blissful feeling of being in love and taking the good with the bad in a relationship. Her sweet sentiment combined with a super-upbeat melody makes this song the perfect bop for when you're feeling butterflies or feeling on top of the world.

What's a romantic gesture that seems simple but means a lot?

_____
_____
_____
_____

What's a memory or a fantasy of this kind of scenario for you?

_____
_____
_____
_____
_____
_____
_____
_____

#56 Wear Cowboy Boots

Go back to Taylor's country music roots and put on those cowboy boots. A style that's iconic and timeless, cowboy boots will always have a place in fashion.

What's so legendary about Taylor's country style?

_____
_____
_____
_____
_____
_____

What about wearing cowboy boots gives you a boost of confidence?

_____
_____
_____
_____
_____
_____
_____
_____
_____
_____

73

#57 Get Your Boating License

In "no body, no crime" off of *evermore*, Taylor sings "Good thing my daddy made me get a boating license when I was fifteen." (This is also an allusion to something Rachel Green says in an episode of Taylor's favorite show, *Friends*!) Take this as a hint from Taylor that everyone should know how to captain a boat. Have you ever been in these boats?

◯ Sailboat
◯ Fishing boat
◯ Yacht
◯ Speedboat

What would the best part of captaining a boat be?

_____
_____
_____
_____
_____
_____
_____
_____

#58 Catch Up on the Classics: *The Scarlet Letter*

The Scarlet Letter by Nathaniel Hawthorne

Taylor sneaks literary references into many of her songs. The lyric "I was a Scarlet Letter" in "Love Story" off of *Fearless* refers to the Hawthorne novel. In the book, the main character, Hester Prynne, is forced to wear a red letter "A" on her clothing as a punishment. Nowadays, the phrase 'wearing a scarlet letter' usually describes a person placed under an unfair spotlight for something the public thinks they've done wrong.

Y/N Read the book

Y/N Watched the movie

Imagine it through Taylor's eyes and write down your thoughts.

_____
_____
_____
_____
_____
_____
_____

#59 Write a Breakup Song

No one does it better than Taylor. If you were to write a breakup song in her style, which era would you use? Get the lyrics or ideas of your breakup song going here.

#60 Find Her Easter Eggs

If you think you've found all of Taylor's sneaky clues and hidden Easter eggs, you're probably in for a surprise. She's been teasing her fans with clues since Day 1, capitalizing random letters in her song titles to form phrases to decode. Since then, she's dropped breadcrumbs literal *years* ahead of album releases, created fun puzzles to unlock, and teased fans with will-she-won't-she hints about what's to come.

What are your favorite T-Swift Easter eggs?

What's something you've found that you think most people missed?

#61 Turn Up that Location Ballad

A gimme. It is a scientific fact that Swifties now only pronounce the Sunshine State with tremendous bravado, as in, "Florida!!!" And no self-respecting fan has rolled up to, landed in, or wandered around certain locations without immediately using the relevant T-Swift songs as the background music for social media. Raise a gel pen if you've done it or plan to! Check off whether you have been to the places associated with these songs and used her music as a background track, or save this page for the day when you eventually will.

Upon arrival

- ○ "Welcome to New York" (*1989*)
- ○ "London Boy" (*Lover*)
- ○ "Florida!!!" (*The Tortured Poets Department*)

After being inconvenienced

- ○ "Fresh Out the Slammer" (*The Tortured Poets Department*)

When departing

- ○ "So Long, London" (*The Tortured Poets Department*)

#62 Make a Taylor Swift Vision Board

Every Swiftie needs one. Choose imagery from your favorite Taylor eras and from snaps of her being iconic on the red carpet or out on the town. Let her inspire you to be your most authentic self and find excitement in what's ahead. What's so Tay about your future days?

I'm making a . . .

◯ Digital board—portability is key

◯ Physical board—give me all the magazine cutouts

Here's my vision for what's yet to come:

#63 Go Full Taylor Glam

Taylor figured out her makeup routine real quick, and for that, the Swifties are grateful. Because now fans know exactly how to pull off the natural look in a comfy cardigan as much as they do a snakeskin-print on a night out. If you haven't tried out her most iconic looks, do it now. If you have, you know the drill: check off those Swiftie boxes and keep it up!

Taylor Beauty Looks

- [x] Red lipstick
- [x] Black lipstick
- [x] Cat eye ("sharp enough to kill a man")
- [x] Winged eye
- [x] Bejeweled eyes
- [x] Gold freckles
- [x] All natural

#64 Be Generous with Your Time

Taylor Swift is a literal billionaire. It's hard to wrap your head around how much money that is, but it's not just life-changing for one person; it has the power to change the lives of whole communities. Taylor has been known to generously give away more than 12 percent of her income each year, which works out to be hundreds of millions of dollars toward disaster relief, food pantries, animal rescue foundations, women's shelters, GoFundMe fundraisers, hospitals, fans' rent and medical bills, ultra-generous bonuses for her Eras Tour crew on every level, and more.

But what's also inspiring about Taylor is that she's generous with her time. She visits hospitals and fundraisers, shows up to fans' personal events, makes handcrafted notes and crafts, and makes sure her voice is the tide that lifts all boats and not just her own. No matter how busy a person feels, there's always a way to stop and give someone who needs it your time.

How could you be generous with your time?

_____

_____

Who has helped you in this way even when they could have used their time differently?

_____

_____

_____

#65 Take a Taylor-Inspired Road Trip

Test out those tires and your playlists with a cross-country road trip. In the Taylor Swift multiverse, there's no end to the number of routes you could take because she namedrops so many different places in her songs and music videos. (If you're not careful, you may never leave New York.) But if Miss Americana were to guide a tour from sea to shining sea, you know it'd be a good one. Get your wheels turning about which route you'd take.

- ◯ Westerly, Rhode Island, to explore the quaint town near Taylor's beach hideaway
- ◯ Oheka Castle, Huntington, New York, to see the estate featured in the "Blank Space" music video
- ◯ Georgia so you can play "Tim McGraw" on repeat
- ◯ The marshlands of North Carolina to pay homage to "Carolina" from *Where the Crawdads Sing*
- ◯ Nashville, Tennessee, to visit Taylor's country roots
- ◯ Las Vegas, Nevada, so you can sing the "Vegas acrobat" line from the clean version of "Karma" in the right location
- ◯ Los Angeles, California, because obviously

#66 Take Polaroids

Taylor loves a Polaroid. The album art for 1989 is made up of instant Polaroid photos. In her song "New Year's Day," off of *Reputation*, she sings about Polaroids left on the hardwood floor. Tap into your inner Tay-grapher and snap a few of your own in a Taylor-inspired photo shoot. Paste or tape your favorites below.

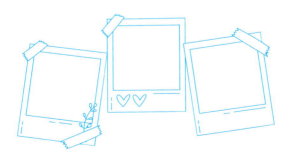

#67 Go to a Christmas Tree Farm

Taylor is full of charm, but one extra sparkle in her personal history is that she grew up on a Christmas tree farm in Pennsylvania. During the winter holiday season, get yourself lost in the aromatic haze of rows and rows of Christmas trees!

- ◯ Snap a photo against the trees
- ◯ Sip hot cocoa
- ◯ Remember the first fall of snow ("and how it glistened as it fell")
- ◯ Make wishes for an enchanting New Year

#68 Catch Up on the Classics: *The Sun Also Rises*

The Sun Also Rises by Ernest Hemingway

Taylor sneaks literary references into many of her songs. Taylor sings, "And isn't it just so pretty to think" in "invisible string" off of *folklore*. The final line and one of Hemingway's most famous quotes is, "Isn't it pretty to think so?"

Y/N Read the book

Y/N Watched the movie

Imagine it through Taylor's eyes and write down your thoughts.

_____
_____
_____
_____
_____
_____
_____
_____

#69 Turn a Skeptic into a Swiftie

The haters have been around as long as Taylor has been making music, but no one is safe from her ability to turn a cynic's frown upside down. Taylor's tireless ability to perfect her craft and reinvent what's expected of her means there's always a hater who can be turned into a Taylor lover. If you have a Swift skeptic in your life, which songs from her discography are destined to turn them into a Swiftie?

1.
2.
3.
4.
5.
6.
7.
8.
9.
10.
11.
12.
13.

#70 Do Something Someone Says You Can't Do

When Taylor was first starting out, she gave an interview in which she couldn't hide her exasperation for someone who dared tell her she couldn't do something. Taylor described asking one of her guitar instructors the difference between a six-string and a twelve-string guitar. She recalls him saying, "I don't even need to answer that for you because there's no way that you'll be able to play a twelve-string guitar at your age." Energized to do exactly that, she picked out her twelve-string, waited until Christmas to get it, and played it until her fingers bled.

What's something you admire about Taylor for doing in spite of the odds?

_____

_____

When has someone underestimated you?

_____

_____

_____

What do you know you can do that others think you can't?

_____

_____

_____

#71 Write a Poem

Take a leaf out of Taylor's *The Tortured Poets Department* manuscript. Write a poem here.

#72 Catch Up on the Classics: "The Road Not Taken"

"The Road Not Taken" by Robert Frost

Taylor sneaks literary references into many of her songs. Taylor references this famous poem not once, but twice in her discography. In "The Outside" off of her debut album, she sings "I tried to take the road less traveled by," which echoes the second-to-last line of Frost's poem. Later, on *evermore*, she sings "And the road not taken looks real good now" in her song "'tis the damn season."

Y/N Read the poem

Imagine it through Taylor's eyes and write down your thoughts.

#73 Do Something Bad

(But not that bad.) Do something "bad" that feels totally out of character. In Taylor's song, "I Did Something Bad," on *Reputation*, she sings about the thrill of doing something no one expects her to do, of having confidence, and of being two steps ahead of everyone.

What's something bad that's felt so *good*?

#74 Have a Merry Swiftmas

Taylor loves the thirteen days of Swiftmas. Throughout her career, she has sent fans hand-painted cards, personalized gifts, and even snow globes featuring the *Lover* house that later became a set design of her sensational Eras Tour. Write out the surprise gifts you'd like to give to people you care about, or even to perfect strangers. Are they handmade cards and crafts, or something else?

1. ___
2. ___
3. ___
4. ___
5. ___
6. ___
7. ___
8. ___
9. ___
10. ___
11. ___
12. ___
13. ___

#75 Use a Typewriter

Taylor may make fun of typewriters in her song, "The Tortured Poets Department," but you'll find her typing away on one during the music video for "Fortnight." If you had access to a typewriter, what are the lyrics, ideas, or dreams would you type out?

#76 Speak Exclusively in Taylor's Vocabulary

Speak more Taylor! Write out the definitions of these words or find the lyrics they are associated with.

FORTNIGHT ("Fortnight")

_____

MALADIES ("How Did It End?")

_____

GAUCHE ("The Last Great American Dynasty")

_____

AURORAS ("The Lakes")

_____

CRESTFALLEN ("champagne problems")

_____

INCANDESCENT ("Ivy")

_____

PETULANCE ("Down Bad")

_____

REVELRY ("But Daddy I Love Him")

_____

RIVULETS ("My Boy Only Breaks His Favorite Toys")

_____

CLANDESTINE ("illicit affairs")

_____

HEATH ("So Long, London")

_____

BEREFT ("How Did It End?")

_____

SABOTEURS ("But Daddy I Love Him")

_____

ESOTERIC ("The Black Dog")

_____

CALAMITOUS ("The Lakes")

_____

TORRID ("The Manuscript")

_____

SANCTIMONIOUSLY ("But Daddy I Love Him")

_____

ALSO-RAN ("The Smallest Man Who Ever Lived")

_____

MACHIAVELLIAN ("Mastermind")

_____

TENDRILS ("But Daddy I Love Him")

_____

_____

#77 Listen to Songs Taylor Wrote but Didn't Sing

Taylor dominates the charts, but it's not always her name that's associated with these dominating hits. She penned or wrote alongside the artists who performed the songs below. Have you heard them all?

◯ "This Is What You Came For" performed by Calvin Harris featuring Rihanna

◯ "You'll Always Find Your Way Back Home" performed by Miley Cyrus

◯ "Better Man" performed by Little Big Town

◯ "Best Days of Your Life" performed by Kelly Pickler

◯ "Babe" performed by Sugarland

#78 Catch Up on the Classics: *A Tale of Two Cities*

A Tale of Two Cities by Charles Dickens

Taylor sneaks literary references into many of her songs. Taylor plays off of Dickens' famous line in "Getaway Car" off of *Reputation* when she says, "It was the best of times, it was the worst of crimes."

Y/N Read the book

Y/N Watched the movie

Y/N Saw the musical

Imagine it through Taylor's eyes and write down your thoughts.

_____
_____
_____
_____
_____
_____
_____

#79 Make Cats Your Whole Personality

Meredith Grey, Olivia Benson, Benjamin Button—these aren't just the names of television and film characters; they're the luckiest cats in the world. Taylor totes her feline companions everywhere, and they more than certainly get the VIP treatment.

If you have a cat or plan to adopt one, what Swiftie-style names are you giving this member of the itty-bitty kitty committee?

_____
_____
_____

What is it about Taylor's affection for her cats that's just so relatable?

_____
_____
_____
_____
_____
_____
_____
_____
_____
_____

#80 Leave the Christmas Lights Up 'Til January

Fall into Taylor's dreamy attitude from her song "Lover." Let the holiday season float across your calendar like snowflakes, and enjoy the twinkly lights for as long as you can. Near the twinkly lights below, write out your favorite ways to relax during the holiday season.

#81 Write a Revenge Fantasy

Taylor loves a little revisionist history, but she *really* loves reimagining comeuppance. From songs like "Better than Revenge" and "Look What You Made Me Do" to "Karma" and "Vigilante Sh*t," this is a girl who knows how to use storytelling as catharsis. The best thing about revenge fantasies is that you can vent frustrations or imagine karma circling back without actually doing anything you'd regret.

What's your revenge fantasy?

#82 Embrace the Snakes

Reputation was the album that brought Taylor back from the brink of being canceled "within an inch of her life." When a celebrity scandal led people to bully her social media with snake emojis, accusing her of being untrustworthy, Taylor latched onto this serpentine imagery and made it all her own. Now snakes are a symbol of taking back her power.

Name a time when you flipped the narrative on something negative and turned it into a positive.

_____
_____
_____
_____
_____
_____
_____
_____
_____
_____
_____
_____
_____
_____

#83 Take on an English Accent

She loves an Englishman! If you couldn't tell from some of her past dating choices, then maybe you heard it in her lyrics. Taylor sings "First I saw the dimples and then I heard the accent" in her song, "London Boy." Spend a day speaking in an English accent for fun and see what happens. Record your experience here.

#84 Get to Know that James Dean Daydream

Taylor sings about a past love having "that James Dean daydream" look in his eyes in the song "Style" off of 1989. James Dean was an actor famous for his brooding looks and untimely death. His memory has become one of an attractive enigma, and he's been referenced in books, film, and music ever since.

What do you know about James Dean?

_____

_____

_____

_____

_____

_____

Have you seen these James Dean films?

Y/N *East of Eden* (1955)

Y/N *Rebel Without a Cause* (1955)

Y/N *Giant* (1956)

#85 Read All the Books Beside Your Bed

In the song "Paper Rings" off of *Lover*, Taylor sings "Went home and tried to stalk you on the internet / now I've read all the books beside your bed." In these lines, she's describing the before-and-after of meeting someone for the first time and being comfortable in a relationship with them. But let's be real. Relationship or not, there is always a stack of books to be read.

What's beside your bed? What books could you read that someone else recommended?

#86 Offset Your Carbon Footprint

Taylor was criticized in the media for contributing to pollution with the use of her private jet. There are reasons for this—it would be difficult for Taylor Swift to safely fly commercial airlines, and regular travelers would be guaranteed to experience delays. But one of Taylor's best qualities is her ability to listen and react. She heard this criticism and immediately adjusted her use of her private jets, and she purchased twice the carbon offsets to make up for the CO_2 emissions she would produce during the Eras Tour.

CO_2 emissions are pollution from carbon-emitting vehicles like airplanes, cars, and trains. Buying carbon offsets is like a charitable donation for the future. The money goes to programs that help balance these emissions, like tree-planting endeavors that help put oxygen back into the air.

In what ways can you help offset your carbon footprint?

- Buy carbon offsets
- Plant trees
- Use renewable energy
- Use electric or hybrid vehicles
- Take public transportation
- Be conscientious of your power usage with small gestures like turning off electricity when you're not using it
- Use a refillable water bottle

#87 Catch Up on the Classics: *A Wrinkle in Time*

A Wrinkle in Time by Madeleine L'Engle

Taylor sneaks literary references into many of her songs. She alludes to the passage of time in a relationship, and her partner's smile, when she says, "A wrinkle in time like the crease by your eyes" in "Hits Different" off of *Midnights*.

Y/N Read the book

Y/N Watched the movie

Imagine it through Taylor's eyes and write down your thoughts.

_____
_____
_____
_____
_____
_____
_____
_____
_____

#88 Learn Words in Other Languages

HOLA

Taylor Swift's Eras Tour visited twenty-one countries and fifty-one cities across five continents. During the song "We Are Never Ever Getting Back Together," her famously charming back-up dancer, Kam Saunders, would change the lyric "Like Ever" to a phrase related to the city or country they were in. In Mexico, he shouted, "like *nunca*" ("like never"), and in Japan, it was "*areinai*" ("impossible"). Taylor learns simple phrases to communicate wherever she goes, showing a respect for the people and culture of the host city she's visiting.

What Swiftie-friendly phrases can you learn?

1. _____
2. _____
3. _____
4. _____
5. _____
6. _____
7. _____
8. _____
9. _____
10. _____
11. _____
12. _____
13. _____

NI HAO

#89 Watch a Magic Show

In 2009, Taylor Swift appeared at the Academy of Country Music Awards. But she didn't just walk out on stage. With the help of David Copperfield, she magically appeared inside an empty elevator. This is not the only time Taylor has performed with magicians, and she's even been the subject of the "impossible sawing" trick. How do you make the magic happen?

- ⟨✗⟩ See a magic show
- ⟨✗⟩ Favorite magic trick:_____
- ⟨✗⟩ Learn a magic trick:_____
- ⟨✗⟩ Learn to juggle

#90 Write a Heartfelt Song

If Taylor's taught us anything, it's that songwriting can help you process emotions and transport you to new places. Whether you're writing "Our Song" on a napkin or something that's more meaningful to you, write a song the Taylor way here.

#91 Cheer On Your Favorite Football Team

The Taylor Effect is for everyone. American football has had a boost in the number of people watching ever since Taylor started attending more games. Whether you're a Kansas City Chiefs fan, a Philadelphia Eagles fan, or you root for your home team, you might catch a few seconds of Swiftie screen time. Get dressed up in your Sunday football finest and cheer with the intensity of Taylor watching the Super Bowl.

My Team:

_____

Y/N Saw my team in real life

Y/N Watched from home

Y/N Wore a red lip

Y/N Did a touchdown dance

#92 Catch Up on the Classics: *Alice's Adventures in Wonderland*

Alice's Adventures in Wonderland by Lewis Carroll

Taylor sneaks literary references into many of her songs. The vault track "Wonderland" from *1989* is themed around the classic work of literature. Taylor sings about falling down a rabbit hole and what happens to "curious minds," which echoes the famous phrase "curiouser and curiouser" from the novel. She talks about going "mad," just like the novel's famous line, "we're all mad here," and she sings about her lover's "Cheshire cat smile," just like that of the mischievous Cheshire cat in the book.

Y/N Read the book

Y/N Watched the movie

Y/N Saw the musical

Imagine it through Taylor's eyes and write down your thoughts.

_____
_____
_____
_____

#93 Stand Up for LGBTQ+ Friends and Strangers

Taylor stands for kindness and for supporting others. In her song, "You Need to Calm Down" off of *Lover*, she shouts "Shade never made anybody less gay" before breaking into an upbeat chorus. This pastel and peppy song isn't just a fun bop—it's a reminder that giving off hate and bad energy to someone you think is different from you will never change who they are. It's just toxic.

How have you supported friends or how have friends supported you?

_____
_____
_____
_____

What's the best way to use your voice to positive effect and to show your love?

_____
_____
_____
_____
_____
_____
_____
_____

#94 Memorize Her Dance Routines

The Eras Tour had Taylor performing rigorous dance routines for three-and-a-half hours every night. She said she wanted to be so over-rehearsed that she didn't have to think about it while she was performing. If you watch videos from early performances and ones from her final shows, you'll see how much more comfortable she got throughout the tour.

In her early career, she wasn't always comfortable dancing—and critics made sure she knew it. But Blondie knows how to pivot. The "Shake It Off" music video was a self-aware, tongue-in-cheek showcase of her dancing awkwardness.

Which dance routine do you know or want to learn?

_____
_____
_____

How hard or easy are these routines to learn?

_____
_____
_____
_____
_____
_____
_____

#95 Use "All Too Well (10 Minute Version)" as a Timer

Swifties around the world have started using Taylor's song off of *Red* as a way to manage their time. Think of most hobbies or activities, and you'll find that ten minutes is the perfect amount of time to get a lot of magic done. Try listening to the extended version of "All Too Well" to your benefit the next time you have a short task or a long task that can be divided into ten-minute increments.

- Bake cookies
- Meditate
- Read an article
- Take a walk
- Organize
- Ugly cry
- Do a workout
- Run a 10-minute mile
- Run a marathon (that's listening to "All Too Well" 26.2 times!)

(Your Version):

_____

_____

_____

#96 Dedicate a Song

There's a Taylor song for everyone and everything. Dedicate a song and the lyrics that hit home for you to someone or something in each of these categories.

MEMORY

Song:

Dedicated to:

Where the lyrics hit:

The Reason:

LOVE

Song:

Dedicated to:

Where the lyrics hit:

The Reason:

BAD EX

Song:

Dedicated to:

Where the lyrics hit:

The Reason:

GOOD EX

Song:

Dedicated to:

Where the lyrics hit:

The Reason:

FRIEND

Song: _____

Dedicated to: _____

Where the lyrics hit: _____

The Reason: _____

FAMILY

Song: _____

Dedicated to: _____

Where the lyrics hit: _____

The Reason: _____

TREPIDATION

Song: _____

Dedicated to: _____

Where the lyrics hit: _____

The Reason: _____

GOAL OR ACHIEVEMENT

Song: _____

Dedicated to: _____

Where the lyrics hit: _____

The Reason: _____

#97 Crash a Party

Make a splash. In the song "Who's Afraid of Little Old Me" off of *The Tortured Poets Department*, Taylor refers to her ghostly-self going out to "crash the party like a record scratch." While you don't necessarily have to make a screaming entrance, go out to a party or event you'd ordinarily be nervous to attend or where you feel like you don't belong. Channel that Taylor confidence and be your most authentic self!

Which songs boost your confidence?

#98 Catch Up on the Classics: *Rebecca*

Rebecca by Daphne du Maurier

Taylor sneaks literary references into many of her songs. Taylor has said that she was inspired by *Rebecca* when writing "tolerate it" off of *evermore*. The line, "Use my best colors for your portrait," alludes to the narrator dressing like her husband's favorite portrait to try to impress him.

Y/N Read the book

Imagine it through Taylor's eyes and write down your thoughts.

_____
_____
_____
_____
_____
_____
_____
_____
_____
_____

#99 Drop Your Own Clues Before Making a Big Announcement

The queen of breadcrumbing, the empress of Easter eggs; Taylor makes dropping hints a full-time job. At her release of *All Too Well: The Short Film* at the 2022 Tribeca Film Festival, she commented, "People often greatly underestimate how much I will inconvenience myself to prove a point."

Bring this energy to your next big thing. What's your big announcement? How would you scatter hints?

#100 Listen to Taylor's Latest Album

Blondie never stops writing, and for this, Swifties are eternally in awe. Whether it's a rerecord *(Taylor's Version)* or a brand-new album, write out the track list here and rate your favorites. Sad songs, mad songs, happy songs, and bangers—the tip of Taylor Swift's pen is a wellspring of material that makes fans feel seen. Her lyrics dig deep and inspire, giving Swifties something to hold onto throughout the ups and downs. Listen to this album like you're studying it and revel in this new sound.

ALBUM TITLE
_____

TRACK LIST

○ _____ ○ _____
○ _____ ○ _____
○ _____ ○ _____
○ _____ ○ _____
○ _____ ○ _____
○ _____ ○ _____
○ _____ ○ _____
○ _____ ○ _____
○ _____ ○ _____
○ _____ ○ _____

#101 Make a Song-of-the-Day Calendar

Taylor has penned and sung nearly 300 songs and shows no sign of stopping, so it won't be too long until there is a unique song for every day of the year. But until then, repeats are always welcome. Start by creating a calendar to map out one song you want to hear each day of the year. Consider filling in birthdays, holidays, and special occasions first, ensuring you'll start those important days off on the right foot, Taylor style!

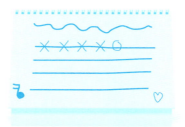

January

1.
2.
3.
4.
5.
6.
7.
8.
9.
10.
11.
12.
13.
14.
15.
16.
17.
18.
19.
20.
21.
22.
23.
24.
25.
26.
27.
28.
29.
30.
31.

February

1.
2.
3.
4.
5.
6.
7.
8.
9.
10.
11.
12.
13.
14.
15.
16.
17.
18.
19.
20.
21.
22.
23.
24.
25.
26.
27.
28.
29.

March

1.
2.
3.
4.
5.
6.
7.
8.
9.
10.
11.
12.
13.
14.
15.
16.
17.
18.
19.
20.
21.
22.
23.
24.
25.
26.
27.
28.
29.
30.
31.

April

1.
2.
3.
4.
5.
6.
7.
8.
9.
10.
11.
12.
13.
14.
15.
16.
17.
18.
19.
20.
21.
22.
23.
24.
25.
26.
27.
28.
29.
30.

May

1.
2.
3.
4.
5.
6.
7.
8.
9.
10.
11.
12.
13.
14.
15.
16.
17.
18.
19.
20.
21.
22.
23.
24.
25.
26.
27.
28.
29.
30.
31.

June

1.
2.
3.
4.
5.
6.
7.
8.
9.
10.
11.
12.
13.
14.
15.
16.
17.
18.
19.
20.
21.
22.
23.
24.
25.
26.
27.
28.
29.
30.

July

1.
2.
3.
4.
5.
6.
7.
8.
9.
10.
11.
12.
13.
14.
15.
16.
17.
18.
19.
20.
21.
22.
23.
24.
25.
26.
27.
28.
29.
30.
31.

August

1.
2.
3.
4.
5.
6.
7.
8.
9.
10.
11.
12.
13.
14.
15.
16.
17.
18.
19.
20.
21.
22.
23.
24.
25.
26.
27.
28.
29.
30.
31.

September

1.
2.
3.
4.
5.
6.
7.
8.
9.
10.
11.
12.
13.
14.
15.
16.
17.
18.
19.
20.
21.
22.
23.
24.
25.
26.
27.
28.
29.
30.

October

1.
2.
3.
4.
5.
6.
7.
8.
9.
10.
11.
12.
13.
14.
15.
16.
17.
18.
19.
20.
21.
22.
23.
24.
25.
26.
27.
28.
29.
30.
31.

November

1.	11.	21.
2.	12.	22.
3.	13.	23.
4.	14.	24.
5.	15.	25.
6.	16.	26.
7.	17.	27.
8.	18.	28.
9.	19.	29.
10.	20.	30.

December

1.	12.	23.
2.	13.	24.
3.	14.	25.
4.	15.	26.
5.	16.	27.
6.	17.	28.
7.	18.	29.
8.	19.	30.
9.	20.	31.
10.	21.	
11.	22.